D0901726

The Ashes of Love

THE ASHES OF LOVE

SAYINGS ON THE

ESSENCE OF NON-DUALITY

RUPERT SPIRA

SAHAJA

SAHAJA PUBLICATIONS

PO Box 887, Oxford OX1 9PR
www.sahajapublications.com

Copyright © Rupert Spira 2016

First published by Non-Duality Press 2013
Second edition by Sahaja Publications 2016

All rights reserved

No part of this book shall be reproduced or transmitted
in any form or by any means, electronic or mechanical, including
photocopying, recording, or by any information
retrieval system, without written permission of the publisher

Designed by Rob Bowden
Printed and bound in China by Toppan Leefung Printing Limited

ISBN 978-0-9929726-1-5

Be only Being
Know only Knowing
Love only Loving

How strange.

We can burn.

How strange and stunning: we can burn from top to bottom and yet find ourselves in fullness.

Each stanza in this book is a blazing firebrand. To really come close, trusting and open, is to torch the jumble of beliefs and delusions that sustained us in quiet desperation, which we had finally considered inevitable. Each stanza in this book burns what we are not and reveals what we are.

*   *   *

We are freedom itself, joy without a cause and peace without an enemy. Furthermore, how striking: never ever have we been limited in the first place.

This book is a distillation of penetrating statements gleaned from the numerous teachings of Rupert Spira: at times borrowing the musicality of a haiku, the terseness of a pith instruction or the persuasive power of an oration. But no matter its shape, each one bears the treasure of a full teaching.

We can only marvel at the simple and effortless nature of this rediscovery of the truth within ourselves. For there is nothing to do; it is done without us, in the simple releasing of all that can be released. In fact, we see that the greatest effort lies in the ceaseless creation and maintenance of an illusion, the illusion of believing oneself to be a separate entity in the face of our actual experience of undivided and universal identity.

In this way, the baseless ideas and beliefs we took on, unquestioningly, are burnt to a cinder, and their cremation is felt as a dissolution. Without our really noticing, the understanding spreads through us and takes full possession of the territory in a broad sweep that is not a movement of the mind but a wave of love.

For love is fully present here. Love is the main character in this book, because it is love that is the core of what we are.

Rupert Spira is an artist. He sculpts words into condensed forms of pure intelligence to which there is nothing to be added or removed. He sculpts our understanding until it becomes pure light, pure flame.

Truth seekers familiar with his teaching will find its essence here: concise, sharp as a diamond, overwhelming with its awesome higher reasoning, whilst bathing us in unconditional love. Others will be struck by the clarity and profundity of Reality as conveyed by this master of Advaita, and illumined by the glimpse of an inner revolution.

Monique Proulx

JANUARY 2013

Translated by Ellen Emmet and Caroline Seymour

Awareness and the Light of Pure Knowing

In *The Ashes of Love*, either the word 'Awareness' or the phrase 'the light of pure Knowing' is used to denote our true nature. Although these both relate to the same non-objective experience – the knowing of our own Being as it essentially is – and are therefore identical, they are used in two different contexts to indicate different stages of understanding. Below is a description of these two stages, clarifying the context in which the words appear in this book.

From the conventional point of view, experience is believed to consist of two essential elements: (1) a subject – the body/mind – and (2) an object – things, others and the world. For this reason, we could call this view of experience Conventional Duality, in which the subject-object relationship is implicit.

In Conventional Duality, the body/mind – the subject of experience – is believed to be joined to things, others and the world – the objects of experience – by an act of knowing, feeling or perceiving. As such, the body/mind is considered to be *aware*, and 'things, others and the world' are considered to be what 'I', the body/mind, am *aware of*.

This belief is the fundamental presumption upon which our world culture is based, and it is enshrined in our language in phrases such as, 'I know such and such', 'I love you', 'I see the tree'. In each case, there is a subject – 'I' – knowing, feeling or perceiving an object – 'you' or 'it'. In fact, so embedded is this belief into the fabric of our culture, that most people do not consider it a belief at all and take it, instead, unquestioningly, as a fact of absolute truth.

As a first step towards an understanding of the true nature of our experience, the non-dual teaching points out that it is not 'I', *the body/mind*, that is aware of things, others and the world, but rather 'I', *Awareness*, that is aware of the body and mind, as well as things, others and the world. As such, the body and mind are understood to be *objects* of experience, not the *subject*.

In this case, it is understood that the subject or knower of experience is not made of anything objective, such as a thought, image, feeling, sensation or perception. It is simply present and aware, and is therefore referred to as 'Awareness'. In the word 'Awareness', the suffix '-ness' means 'the state, being or presence of'. Thus, 'Awareness' means 'the state of being aware', or simply 'being aware' or 'aware Being'.

Being devoid of all objective characteristics, the subject of experience – pure Awareness – is said to be inherently empty: empty of thoughts, images, feelings, sensations and perceptions; transparent, colourless, formless, imperceptible and, ultimately, inconceivable; although if we are to speak or write of the ultimate nature of experience, we have to consent to conceive of it provisionally.

The process through which we discover that it is not 'I', the *body/mind*, that is aware of things, others and the world, but 'I', *Awareness*, that is aware of the body and mind, as well as things, others and the world, is sometimes referred to as *neti neti*: I am not this, not this. I am not my thoughts; I am *aware* of my thoughts. I am not my feelings; I am *aware* of my feelings. I am not my bodily sensations; I am *aware* of my bodily sensations. I am not my perceptions – sights, sounds, tastes, textures and smells – I am *aware* of these.

As such, *neti neti* is a process of discrimination or exclusion, through which we move from the belief that I am 'something' – a mixture of a body and a mind – to the understanding that I am 'nothing' (not-a-thing) – not a thought, image, feeling, sensation or perception.

Thus, the culmination of the path of *neti neti* – the Path of Exclusion – is to know our Self as pure Awareness. However, this process has not, as yet, told us anything about the *nature* of Awareness, other than that it is simply present and aware. As such, it is not what is traditionally referred to as awakening or enlightenment. Awakening or enlightenment is not just the revelation of the *presence* of Awareness – although that is a first step – but of its *nature*.

*   *   *

To move from the understanding that Awareness is present and aware to the realisation of its true nature requires, in most cases, some exploration. However, who or what could explore or know Awareness? Only Awareness is aware and, therefore, only Awareness can know anything about itself. Thus, to explore Awareness means to be aware of Awareness. However, in order to be aware of itself, Awareness doesn't need to know something new. Just by being itself, Awareness is already and always naturally, effortlessly aware of itself, just as the sun naturally and effortlessly illuminates itself simply by being itself.

Thus, truly to enquire into our essential nature, although almost always initiated by a process of thinking and questioning, is, ultimately, simply to abide knowingly as our essential Being of pure Awareness. In this process, the outward- or object-facing mind is divested of its object and, having nothing to focus on or attach itself to, flows back naturally, effortlessly and spontaneously to its source as pure Awareness, and abides as that knowingly.

It is in this abidance as our essential nature of pure Awareness that the memory of our ever-present and unlimited nature dawns – the memory of our eternal, infinite Being. Of course, this is not a memory 'of something'. However, the word 'memory' is appropriate because this knowing of our own Being – its knowing of itself as it essentially is – has always been with us and, therefore, is not something that is known anew. It was just *apparently* lost, veiled, overlooked or forgotten.

This memory of our ever-present, unlimited nature is referred to variously in the spiritual traditions as awakening, enlightenment, satori, liberation, illumination, nirvana, resurrection, moksha, bodhi, rigpa, kensho, etc. In all these examples, the same experience is being referred to: the relinquishing of the identification with everything that we previously considered inherent in and essential to our Self. It is referred to in the Zen tradition as *The Great Death*, and is depicted in the Christian religion as the Crucifixion and Resurrection – the dissolution of the limits that thought superimposed upon our Self, and the revelation of its eternal, unlimited nature.

This awakening to our essential nature of ever-present, unlimited Awareness may or may not have an immediate and dramatic effect on the body and mind. In fact, in many cases, this recognition can take place so quietly that the mind may not even notice it to begin with.

I once heard a story in which a student of a well-known Zen master asked him, 'Why don't you ever speak of your enlightenment experience?' At this point the Zen master's wife stood up at the back of the hall and called out, 'Because he never had one!' Others relate becoming so disorientated by the simple recognition of their own essential Being that, for instance, they spend the next two years sitting on a park bench acclimatising!

Either way, the recognition of our true nature is only a halfway stage: the true nature of our Self – pure Awareness – has been recognised as the eternal, infinite subject of all experience, but the objects of the body, mind and world have yet to be incorporated into our new understanding.

At this stage, our true nature has been realised as transcendent Awareness; the witnessing presence of Awareness in the background of all experience; the ever-present, limitless space in which the temporary, limited objects of the body, mind and world appear, and with which they are known; the emptiness in which the fullness of experience arises.

However, from this point of view, experience still consists of a subject – albeit an enlightened one – and an object. The subject – eternal, infinite Awareness – is sometimes likened to an open, empty space like the sky, in which the objects of experience – thoughts, images, feelings, bodily sensations, and perceptions – appear and disappear like clouds. As such, Awareness is still 'something', albeit a transparent, empty 'something'. We are still in the realm of duality – which we might call Enlightened Duality – in which an eternal, infinite subject seems to know a temporary, finite object.

It is in this context that the word 'Awareness' is used in *The Ashes of Love*.

*   *   *

For the peace and happiness that are inherent in the knowing of our own Being – its knowing of itself – to be fully felt and lived in all aspects of life, our enlightened understanding needs to be incorporated into all realms of experience, that is, into the way we think, feel, act, perceive and relate.

Hence, there is a second path – the Path of Inclusion or the Tantric Path – in which the way we think, feel, act, perceive and relate is gradually realigned with our new understanding. In this Path of Inclusion – or, as it is referred to in the Zen tradition, *The Great Rebirth*, and in the Christian tradition, the transfiguration – we discover that our essential nature of pure Awareness is not just present as the *witness* of all experience, but is the very *substance* or *reality* of all experience. As such, it is not just the *background* of experience, but also the *foreground*; not just *transcendent*, but also *immanent*.

In this realisation, duality, that is, the distinction between the subject – pure Awareness – and the objects of the body, mind and world, has collapsed. In fact, it has not collapsed, for it was never really there to begin with. Rather, it has been seen clearly that duality is and has always been utterly non-existent: in reality, there is no self – neither temporary and limited, nor ever-present and unlimited – that *knows*, nor any finite object, other or world that is *known*. There is just pure *Knowing* – one intimate, seamless, indivisible, ever-present, unlimited whole.

It is in this sense that the term 'Knowing' or 'the light of pure Knowing' is used in *The Ashes of Love*: to describe the feeling-understanding that all distinction between an apparent subject and an apparent object, other or world has dissolved, in contrast to the term 'Awareness' or 'pure Awareness', in which there is still an apparent subject and object.

And just as the open, empty sky, in which the objects of the body, mind and world float like clouds, is used as a metaphor for Awareness's relationship to experience, so the metaphor of a screen and an image or movie is used as a metaphor for pure Knowing, in which there is no subject or object.

However, the screen in this metaphor is an aware screen: it is viewing or knowing the images that appear on it, *and* is simultaneously the substance out of which they are made. As such, it knows them as itself, not as objects or others.

In this case, there is no actual, independently existing object on the screen called 'an image'. There are not two things – 'A-dvaita', not-two – screen and image; there is *just* the screen. It is the screen that, vibrating within itself, appears as the image but never becomes or knows anything other than itself.

In the same way pure Knowing, vibrating within itself, takes the shape of thinking, feeling, sensing, seeing, hearing, touching, tasting and smelling, and *seems* to become a mind, body and world, but never truly becomes or knows anything other than itself.

Thus, there are no 'objects' from the point of view of pure Knowing. There are only objects and selves from the illusory point of view of one of the characters in the movie.

The common name for the absence of any distinction between a subject that knows and an object, other or world that is known, is love or beauty. Love is the experience that there are no others; beauty is the experience that there are no objects.

In fact, no word can legitimately be used to describe the reality of experience, which remains unnameable, forever beyond the reach of thought, and yet utterly intimate. It is for this reason that either no words at all or a great many words are used in the attempt to convey this Reality!

*　　*　　*

The Path of Exclusion – I am *not* this, *not* this – takes us from the belief 'I am something' to the understanding 'I am nothing'. The Path of Inclusion – I *am* this, I *am* this – takes us from the understanding 'I am nothing' to the feeling-understanding 'I am everything'.

The Path of Exclusion is a path of discrimination, in which we make a distinction between what is essential to our Self and what is not. The Path of Inclusion is a path of love, in which all such distinctions are seen to be non-existent, and we discover our innate intimacy with all seeming objects and others. This path of love leads to what could be called Embodied Enlightenment, in which the understanding of the true nature of ever-present, unlimited Awareness gradually percolates into all realms of life, permeating and saturating the body, the mind and the world with its light. It is a never-ending process.

From Conventional Duality to Enlightened Duality, we take the Path of Exclusion, the Path of Discrimination; from Enlightened Duality to Embodied Enlightenment, we take the Tantric Path of Inclusion, the Path of Love and Beauty.

These three stages – Conventional Duality, Enlightened Duality and Embodied Enlightenment – are found in all the great spiritual and religious traditions: in Christianity, the crucifixion, resurrection and transfiguration; in the alchemical tradition, discrimination, illumination and transformation; in the Buddhist tradition, samsara, then nirvana, then samsara equals nirvana: first form, then emptiness, then emptiness is form and form is emptiness. As Ramana Maharshi said, 'The world is unreal; only Brahman is real; Brahman is the world.'

First, we discover that all experience appears *in* and is known *by* the open, empty space of Awareness. Then, we discover that Awareness is not just the container and knower but the very *substance* or *reality* of all experience.

As the distinction between Awareness and the apparent objects of the body, mind and world collapses or, more accurately, is seen to be utterly non-existent, it is realised that all we ever know or come in contact with is the *knowing* of experience. In fact, it is not the knowing 'of experience', because experience, independent of Knowing, is never found.

We just know Knowing. However, the 'we' or the 'I' that knows Knowing is not separate or distinct from it. Knowing is not known by something other than itself.

All that is ever known is Knowing, and it is Knowing that knows itself.

There is only the light of pure Knowing.

Rupert Spira
SEPTEMBER 2014

From the viewpoint of the earth, the sun comes and goes, whereas it is, in fact, always present. Likewise, from the viewpoint of the body and mind, our essential nature of pure Awareness comes and goes, but in its own experience of itself, it is ever-present.

All experience is illuminated, or made knowable, by the light of pure Knowing. This Knowing pervades all thoughts, feelings, sensations and perceptions, irrespective of their particular characteristics. We *are* this transparent, unchanging Knowing.

Our Self – luminous, open, empty Awareness – cannot be enlightened. It is already the light that illuminates all experience. Nor can a separate self be enlightened, for when the separate self faces the light of Awareness, it vanishes, just as a shadow does when exposed to the sun.

To invest one's identity and security in something that appears, moves, changes and disappears is the cause of unhappiness.

The separate self is not an entity; it is an activity: the activity of thinking and feeling that our essential nature of pure Awareness shares the limits and the destiny of the body and mind.

Just as a screen is intimately one with all images and, at the same time, free of them, so our true nature of luminous, empty Knowing is one with all experiences and yet, at the same time, inherently free of them.

We are the open, empty, allowing presence of Awareness, in which the objects of the body, mind and world appear and disappear, with which they are known and, ultimately, out of which they are made. Just notice that and be that, knowingly.

When everything that can be let go of is let go of, what remains is what we desire above all else.

In ignorance, I am something; in understanding, I am nothing; in love, I am everything.

Our Self – luminous, empty Awareness – knows no resistance and is, therefore, Peace itself; it seeks nothing and is, thus, Happiness itself; it is intimately one with all appearances and is, as such, pure Love.

The one thing the separate self cannot stand is being clearly seen. To see the separate self clearly is to see its non-existence.

I, open, empty Awareness, am aware of thoughts, feelings, sensations and perceptions but am not made of any of these. All these come, go, move and change, whilst I remain as I am, without birth, death, movement or change – eternal and infinite.

Now is not a moment in time, sandwiched between the two vast spaces of past and future. This present Now is the only Now there is – the eternal Now. It has not come from anywhere and is not going anywhere.

Time and space are thought's way of conceptualising the eternal and infinite nature of Awareness.

Total openness, pure sensitivity, unconditional allowing: this is not something you, as a person, can do; it is what you, as pure Awareness, are.

From the point of view of a finite self, experience consists of a multiplicity and diversity of finite objects and selves, some of which are conceived as 'me', others as 'not me'. From the point of view of experience itself, there is just the seamless intimacy of itself, one indivisible, unnameable whole, always changing in name and form but never changing in essence.

Our essential nature of pure Awareness has no name, but is called by all names; it has no form, but is the substance of all forms.

There are three essential steps on the spiritual path: the first is to notice that one is not a body or a mind, but rather the Awareness in which these appear, and with which they are known; the second is to explore the nature of Awareness and discover that it doesn't share the destiny or the limits of the body and mind – that is, to discover its eternal, infinite nature; and the third is to live a life that is consistent with this understanding.

The separate self is not an entity; it is an activity: the activity of resisting what is present and seeking what is not present.

Just as a moth never touches the flame that it seeks but rather dies in it, so the apparently separate self never finds the peace or happiness for which it longs, but rather dissolves in it. This dissolution *is* the experience of peace and happiness.

There are two possibilities for thought: either to go outwards in the direction of objects or states, in which case it takes the form of suffering, or to go inwards towards the heart of experience, in which case it dissolves in peace.

Be knowingly the inherently peaceful presence of Awareness, and see that this peace is not dependent upon the condition of the mind, body or world, just as a screen is not dependent on the content of the words or the quality of the images that appear on it.

Know yourself as nothing; feel yourself as everything.

Happiness is simply the knowing of our Being as it essentially is – its knowing of itself. The apparent overlooking, veiling or forgetting of our own Being is the root cause of all unhappiness.

Our Self – luminous, open, empty Awareness – cannot be known as an object, but is never not known.

We are the Knowing with which all experience is known, and the Being in all that exists. These apparent two – Knowing and Being – are one in and as our Self.

The Knowing with which the mind seems to know objects, others and the world belongs to our Self, ever-present, unlimited Awareness, just as the light with which the moon illuminates the earth belongs to the sun.

Awareness – the intimacy of our own Being – cannot be known as an object, such as a thought, feeling, sensation or perception, and yet in all of these it is Awareness alone that is truly known, just as the screen is never found in a movie, and yet is all that is truly seen.

Meditation is what we are, not what we do; the separate self is what we do, not what we are.

The entire adventure of the separate self takes place in a little bubble of thought and feeling within Awareness, but Awareness itself never takes the adventure.

Just as a character in a movie is only real from the point of view of that character, so a separate self is only real from its own imaginary point of view.

See thoughts and feelings like a train that enters a station and then leaves; be like the station, not like a passenger.

Experience is not inherently divided into one part that experiences and another that is experienced. It is one indivisible, unnameable, intimate whole. Love and beauty are the names that are given to experience when this intimacy is known and felt. They are the natural condition of all experience, not the particular condition of some experience.

Be neither the knower nor the known, but rather the knowing of experience, and you will find yourself as everyone and everything.

Our essential being of pure Awareness lends its reality to all seeming things, giving them their apparently independent existence, just as a screen lends its reality to the characters and objects in a movie, giving them their own apparently independent existence.

Experience is one seamless, unnameable, intimate whole. It is thought alone that divides this intimacy into an apparent multiplicity and diversity of objects and selves, thereby imagining a 'me' and a 'not me'.

When doing slows down, the thinking that is at its origin is exposed; when thinking dissolves, the feeling that is behind it is uncovered; when feeling subsides, the Being that is at its heart is revealed.

Be knowingly the open, empty, luminous space of Awareness – open, because it allows all appearances of the mind, body and world just as they are; empty because it has no form of its own, but allows all forms within it; and luminous because it is that which illuminates or makes knowable all experience.

To see what the separate self is, is to see that it isn't.

Meditation is neither an activity nor the cessation of an activity. It is to abide knowingly as the empty, open, allowing presence of Awareness, in which all experience appears, with which it is known and, ultimately, out of which it is made.

When we understand that what we deeply long for can never be found in an object, substance, activity, relationship or state, our longing naturally and effortlessly loses its direction and dynamism, flows back to its source, and is revealed as the happiness for which we were in search.

When feeling is divested of the feeler and the felt, it shines as love; when perceiving is divested of the perceiver and the perceived, it shines as beauty.

We cannot know happiness; we can only be it. We cannot be unhappy; we can only know it.

Separate objects and selves only come into existence from the illusory point of view of a separate subject, whilst I, Awareness, who am neither a subject nor an object, and yet the reality of both, am eternally present.

All that is known is the knowing of experience, and we are that Knowing.

To begin with, we seem to be in the world, then the world seems to be in us, and finally the distinction between ourself and the world dissolves.

Look in all experience for that which does not appear, move, change, evolve or disappear, and know yourself as that.

Just as a screen is never truly obscured, let alone harmed, by any image, although it is one with all images, so our essential nature of pure Awareness is never veiled or hurt by any appearance of the body, mind or world, although it is intimately one with all such appearances.

To know the world is to be the world, and to be the world is to love the world.

All that is experienced is experience, but there is no independent self that experiences and no independent object, other or world that is experienced. There is just the experiencing of experience, and it is Experiencing that experiences experience.

Ask your Self, Awareness, what it thinks or feels about any experience, and the response will always be the same, irrespective of the particular quality of that experience: no response!

Happiness is the absence of resistance to what is. It is the highest spiritual practice. However, it is not a practice that can be undertaken by a person; it is the ever-present nature of our Self, Awareness.

When the 'I' of the separate self is relieved of all superimposed thoughts and feelings, it is revealed as the ever-present, unlimited 'I' of pure Awareness.

Identification is always for thought, never for our Self.

Just as one sun is reflected in numerous puddles, each showing a separate image of the same sun, so the unlimited and ever-present light of pure Knowing is reflected in seven billion minds as the feeling 'I am', giving rise to the appearance of seven billion selves.

We normally think that to be a separate self is natural and effortless, and that to be the open, empty presence of Awareness requires effort. In fact, it is the other way round: to be the open, empty presence of Awareness is natural and effortless, but to be a separate self requires a continuous and subtle effort of thinking and feeling.

Don't be a seer; be the seeing. To be a seer is to be someone, somewhere; to be the seeing is to be no one, everywhere.

In understanding, we stand as open, empty Awareness – the witness of all experience; in love, we stand as the light of pure Knowing – the substance of experience.

Experience appears as a reflection of your point of view: from the point of view of a body, it is a collection of objects and selves; from the point of view of a mind, it is all thinking, sensing and perceiving; from the point of view of Awareness, it is only Awareness.

Just as steam, water and ice are all modulations of one substance, so the mind, body and world are all modulations of one Being – the ever-present light of pure Knowing.

I shine as the Knowing in all that is known, just as the sun shines as the light in all that is seen.

I – luminous, open, empty Awareness – am the truth of your Being and am eternally with you, in you, as you, shining quietly at the heart of all experience. Just turn towards Me, and acknowledge Me, and I will take you into Myself.

The mind, body and world wake and sleep in Me – the light of pure Knowing – but I never wake or sleep in them.

When the seeking and resisting that characterise the apparently separate self come to an end, our essential nature of peace and happiness shines as it truly is.

If we want to change our thoughts, we will have to start by changing the universe.

The separate entity thrives on trying to make the mind peaceful, and in doing so only perpetuates the agitation that is at the heart of itself. Leave the mind to be as it is, and remain as you are.

Our Self, the light of pure Knowing, cannot be thought, felt or perceived, but makes all thinking, sensing and perceiving possible.

When happiness is veiled, desire arises. When desire is fulfilled, happiness is revealed. In understanding, we do not allow happiness to be veiled. In ignorance, we seek to fulfil our desires.

That for which all people long is eternally present, shining at the heart of all experience.

Thought gives experience its name, the senses give it its form, but the light of pure Knowing gives it its reality.

Suffering is not the opposite of happiness; it is the veiling of happiness. It is a call from happiness itself, reminding us that we have mistaken our Self for an idea, an image or an object.

The separation between the knower and the known, the experiencer and the experienced, the thinker and the thought, the feeler and the felt, the doer and the deed, never actually occurs. It is made only of the thought that thinks it, and is substantiated in the body as feelings.

Just as the unlimited screen appears limited when it assumes the name and form of a character or object in a movie, but never actually becomes limited, so our Self, Awareness, seems to become temporary and limited when it assumes the form of thinking, sensing and perceiving, but is never truly limited by any of these.

Thoughts and feelings have preferences, make choices, like and dislike, seek and resist, praise and blame, hope and despair, judge and condemn, but our Self, Awareness, that which knows them, does not share their prejudices. Awareness looks on all people and things alike, just as the sun shines on all objects equally.

Attention is Awareness plus an object. Relieved of its focus on an object, attention flows back to its source and knows itself as pure Awareness.

All that is secure in the known is Knowing. All that is safe in experience is Experiencing.

By far the larger part of the apparently separate self exists as a feeling in the body, not just a thought in the mind. Until the non-dual understanding penetrates deeply into the body, though our understanding may be clear, we will continue to feel, act, perceive and relate in ways that betray the apparent existence of a separate self.

Before any thought, sensation or perception tells us anything about a mind, body or world, it first announces the presence of Awareness, in which it appears, with which it is known and, ultimately, out of which it is made. As such, all experience shines with the light of Awareness.

Awareness lives in eternity but dances in time.

Don't lose yourself in thoughts and feelings; let them lose themselves in you.

Just as the moon is, at times, completely, partially or not at all visible, and yet is always the same full moon, so Awareness is fully present at all times and under all circumstances, although the three states of waking, dreaming and sleeping make it seem to appear, move, change and disappear.

For the thought-and-feeling-made self, some experiences are intimate, others not. For the true and only Self of pure Awareness, all experience is equally intimate.

Our Self, Awareness, is like an open, empty, allowing space. As such, we resist nothing, hold nothing, seek nothing. Thus, happiness is our essential nature.

Thoughts are nearly always on a journey into a past or a future, but our essential nature of pure Awareness never takes the journey with them.

Can you separate anyone or anything from experience, and experience from yourself? No? Then don't!

Just as a character in a movie seems to travel the world but never actually leaves the screen, so thought seems to travel into a past and a future but never actually leaves the Now.

An object exists because we think about it; we don't think about it because it exists.

When the 'I' of the apparently separate self is divested of all beliefs and feelings of lack and limitation, it stands revealed as the true and only 'I' of ever-present, unlimited Awareness.

With your mind, know ten thousand things; with your heart, feel only one Reality.

The radical cure for suffering is to see that, like empty space, our essential nature of pure Awareness does not know resistance, and thus does not know suffering.

Know yourself as the seeing, not the seer, and you will find yourself everywhere.

All that is experienced of a mind, body and world is thinking, feeling, sensing, seeing, hearing, tasting, touching and smelling; and all these are made only of the knowing of them. Thus, all that is ever known is Knowing, and it is Knowing that knows Knowing.

The separate, inside self is like a middleman, dividing our essential Being of ever-present, unlimited Awareness from all experience. This division places us in a relationship of conflict, always seeking to hold onto, resist or change the current situation, never letting it be the one thing it always is – just what it is. Without the middleman, the relationship between our Self and all experience is one of natural, effortless intimacy. This intimacy is the experience of love in relation to people and animals, happiness in relation to situations, and beauty in relation to objects.

If separation were real, we would have to get rid of it. However, separation is an illusion. Attempting to get rid of an illusion only asserts its apparent reality, thereby strengthening it.

The mystic investigates himself; the artist and scientist explore the world. If both go far enough they inevitably end up with the same conclusion: that everything and everyone shares the same Reality. It is only because either party doesn't go all the way that there seem to be differences.

Instead of thinking of experience as a collection of objects or nouns, feel only in terms of verbs. Instead of thinking, 'I know such and such', feel, 'There is only knowing and I am that'. Instead of thinking, 'I love you', feel, 'There is only loving and I am that'. Instead of thinking, 'I see the tree', feel, 'There is only seeing and I am that'.

First we imagine an ego, then defend it, then express it, then fulfill it, then try to get rid of it, then welcome it, then understand it, and finally see that it is non-existent at all times.

Just as darkness comes upon the earth when it is turned away from the sun, so the darkness of ignorance comes upon the self when it is turned away from its source, the light of pure Knowing.

Thinking, sensing and perceiving are modulations of pure Knowing, temporary names and forms of our Self. Know, be and love only this Knowing in all experience.

The Knowing with which the past is remembered and the future imagined cannot itself be remembered or imagined.

The only barrier to peace and happiness is the thought that considers the current situation wrong or inadequate. That thought is like a plant that flowers in our feelings, activities and relationships, but has deep roots. It is not enough to pick the flower.

All that is known is Experiencing, and whatever it is that knows Experiencing is utterly, intimately one with it. In fact, it is not even 'one with' it, for there are not really two things there – 'Experiencing' and 'the knowing of it' – to be one with each other. There is just the indivisible, unnameable intimacy of Experiencing, made only of pure Knowing.

I, the light of pure Knowing, never venture out of Myself in order to come into contact with a thought, sensation or perception. I always remain within Myself, and whatever I find in Myself is made only of Myself.

There is no separate, inside self and no separate, outside object, other or world. Rather, there is one seamless, intimate whole, always changing when viewed from the perspective of objects, but never changing when viewed from the perspective of that whole.

An object is the name thought gives to Reality when viewing it from the point of view of a subject. In the absence of that point of view, experience is no longer divided into these two elements – a subject and an object – and all seeming things are experienced as they truly are, eternal and infinite.

The more we explore and penetrate the essential nature of experience, the fewer distinctions we find.

It is only an imaginary inside self that seeks happiness in an outside object, other or world, whilst all the while I, the light of pure Knowing, abide eternally in the peace of My own Being.

To be present in and as all that is seen is to participate in life, not as a fragment amongst other fragments, but as Love, intimately one with all seeming objects and selves.

When the self is relieved of all limitations superimposed upon it by thought, it is revealed as pure Awareness. When the world is relieved of all superimposed limitations, it is revealed as pure Being. These two are identical and we are that.

Looking for happiness in the body, mind or world is like looking for the screen in a movie. The screen doesn't appear *in* the movie, and yet, at the same time, all that is seen in the movie *is* the screen. In the same way that the screen 'hides' in plain view, so happiness 'hides' in all experience.

It is our exclusive interest in objects that gives them their apparently independent reality. When attention shifts from the seen object to pure seeing, the apparently separate reality of the object disappears and its true reality – the light of pure Knowing – shines.

The fact that the current situation is present indicates that Awareness has already fully accepted it. It is only an imaginary self that subsequently resists it. In fact, the imaginary separate self comes into apparent existence *as* that resistance.

To believe that our Self – luminous, open, empty Awareness – shares the limits and the destiny of the mind and body is like believing that the screen shares the limits and the destiny of a character in a movie.

Thoughts, feelings, sensations and perceptions may be agitated or calm but I, the presence of Awareness that knows them, do not share their qualities. I am the luminous, open, empty, aware space that cannot be agitated by any appearance of the mind, body or world, and hence peace is My nature.

Thought divides knowing into a knower and the known, loving into a lover and the beloved, and perceiving into a perceiver and the perceived. As such, it is thought alone that abstracts a subject and an object from the seamless, unnameable intimacy of pure Knowing or Experiencing.

I, the light of pure Knowing, which lives at the heart of all experience, am completely vulnerable and, at the same time, utterly indestructible.

The tragedy and comedy of the human condition is that we spend most of our lives thinking, feeling, acting, perceiving and relating on behalf of a non-existent self.

Matter, mind and Awareness are not three different realities. They are three different ways of seeing one Reality.

Our essential nature of pure Awareness gains or loses nothing from the entire human adventure.

The eternal Now, when seen through the narrow slit of the mind, appears as time. The infinite Here, when seen through the narrow slit of the mind, appears as space.

Just as the sun is always shining but seems to disappear when the earth turns away, so I – the light of pure Knowing – am ever-present and shining brightly in all experience, but seem to disappear when the mind turns its back on Me and looks in the direction of objects and states.

When we treat the world as the face of God, it reveals itself
as such.

As soon as anything appears, Awareness simultaneously knows it, allows it and lets it go.

The recognition of our true nature of ever-present, unlimited Awareness is instantaneous or, more accurately, timeless. The realignment of our thoughts, feelings, activities, perceptions and relationships with this understanding is endless.

Give your mind to whatever comes and goes, but give your heart to that which remains always with you.

Beauty is never seen, but every object is its footprint; love is never felt, but every feeling is its face; understanding is never known, but every thought shines with its light.

Be knowingly the inherently peaceful presence of Awareness, in which thoughts, feelings, sensations and perceptions appear. Allow these to evolve without interference, and if there is interference, simply allow that also. In allowing everything to be exactly as it is from moment to moment, we are, without realising it at first, taking our stand as Awareness.

The only place the separate self cannot stand is Now.

The mind, body or world may lack something, but our Self – luminous, open, empty Awareness, which knows this sense of lack – is inherently free of it. Thus, happiness is its nature.

Love is the inherent intimacy of all experience, in which a subject and an object are never found. Love is not a special relationship; it is the natural condition of *all* relationship.

Just as the sun's light renders all objects visible but is not itself an object, so our Self, the light of pure Knowing, renders all experience knowable, but cannot itself be known as an object.

The self that seeks love is like a moth that seeks a flame.
The flame is all it wants but the one thing it cannot have.

There are three possibilities open to us at every moment: one, to stand as a separate self, which resists what is present and seeks what is not; two, to stand as the open, empty space of Awareness, in which all experience appears and with which it is known; and three, to stand as the light of pure Knowing, out of which all experience is made. Experience will appear in accordance with whichever stand is taken.

Thought imagines a knower and a known, but experience knows only knowing; thought imagines a lover and a beloved, but experience knows only loving; thought imagines a perceiver and the perceived, but experience knows only perceiving.

Just as a person may dream that they grow up, go to school, make friends, get educated, fall in love, get married, find a job, have children, enjoy the pleasures and pains of family life, have grandchildren, get sick, grow old, find themselves surrounded by their family on their deathbed and, as they die, wake up to find that they were peacefully sleeping all along in their bed, so our Self – pure Awareness – experiences the life of the apparently separate self, eternally at rest in its own Being, without ever going anywhere or doing anything.

No activity or inactivity of the mind will make the peace of our true nature more or less present than it is in this very moment.

A separate self doesn't *have* a point of view; it *is* a point of view.

Know nothing; be everything.

Just as the sun cannot know darkness, so I, the light of pure Knowing, cannot know ignorance or separation. Therefore, for Me there is no ignorance, no separate self and no corresponding separate object, other or world. All these are for thought and feeling, not for Myself.

Now does not take place in time; all apparent time takes place Now.

The mind and body are always on a journey, moving and changing, but I, pure Awareness, which knows or is aware of all such movement and change, do not take the journey with them. I do not share their destiny or limits. I never become what they seem to be.

Happiness, which is the simple knowing of our own Being as it essentially is, is not dependent on the conditions of the body, mind or world. It is our ever-present nature. It lies shining quietly in the background of all experience and, when it is recognised, overflows into the foreground, pervading all experience with its qualities.

True prayer is the dissolution of the one who prays and the one who is prayed to, leaving the heart open, naked and melted.

The forgetting or overlooking of our essential Being is never an actual experience for our Self; it is always only a thought or feeling. In other words, our Self – the true and only Self of pure Knowing or Awareness – never truly overlooks or forgets itself. From its own point of view, which is the only real point of view, it eternally knows itself alone.

Psychological suffering is born of the 'I don't like what is present and I want what is not present' thought; as such, suffering is for thought, not for Awareness.

A colourless screen may assume all colours and thus appear as a person, landscape or building, but never actually becomes any of these. Likewise, I, the light of pure Knowing, vibrate within Myself and, as a result, assume all apparently limited names and forms, without ever actually becoming a limited object, self or world.

The mind does not need to be made accepting, choiceless, unjudging or unconditional. I, Awareness, am already and inherently accepting, choiceless, unjudging and unconditional.

The ultimate purpose of life is to find happiness or, for spiritual seekers, to find enlightenment, which is the same thing. However, I, Awareness, am already the happiness and the light for which all seemingly separate selves are in search.

Experience is ever-changing in name and form but never-changing in essence.

Our Self, the light of pure Knowing, is completely empty and, at the same time, the substance out of which the fullness of all experience is made.

All thoughts that revolve around an imaginary inside self leave an echo or imprint in the body. As a result, the body remains a safe refuge for the sense of separation long after the belief in a separate self has dissolved.

I, Awareness, never become a separate self, and the imaginary separate self never becomes Me.

The search for the happiness we deeply long for as an object in the body, mind or world compels it to seem as if hidden.

In fear or resistance, we are pulled towards a past; in desire or seeking, we are propelled towards a future. Resistance and seeking are the two essential forms of the separate self. The only place they cannot stand is Now.

I – luminous, open, empty Awareness – never find Myself in a situation; all situations find themselves in Me.

The projection of an object, other or world 'outside' is the natural and inevitable counterpart to the contraction of a self 'inside'. In the absence of this division of experience, there is just the indivisible, unnameable intimacy of experience.

The light of pure Knowing, which shines in all that is known, doesn't share the changing qualities of the known but is, at the same time, its reality, just as the screen doesn't share the qualities of the image, but is its substance.

There is no substance present in our experience other than the knowing of it, and that Knowing is known by itself alone. Thus, pure Knowing is indivisible and intimate, admitting no distance, separation, self, object or other. It knows, is and loves itself alone.

If we leave thoughts and feelings alone, they will leave us alone.

Experience experiences itself as one seamless, indivisible, unnameable, ever-present whole. It is only thought, which is itself made only of experience, which imagines that experience is fragmented into objects and selves.

In ignorance, I, Awareness, seem to assume the qualities of the mind and body; in understanding, the mind and body assume the qualities of peace and happiness that are inherent in Myself; in love, everything vanishes in Me.

Just as a screen assumes the name and form of an image with which it seems to veil itself, so I, the light of pure Knowing, assume the name and forms of thinking, sensing and perceiving, and appear, as a result, as a mind, body and world. Thus, with My own creativity, I assume a form with which, from the point of view of that form, I seem to veil Myself. However, I am never really veiled from Myself. I am only veiled from the illusory point of view of one of the names and forms that I assume. When I seem to veil Myself from Myself in this way, I am known as Maya.

Our Self, pure Awareness, is at home in the Now; the separate self is at home in time. For this reason, they never meet.

Every object is the footprint of God.

There are three states of waking, dreaming and sleeping only from the point of view of thought. For Awareness, there are not three states; there is the one ever-present Reality of itself in the ever-present Reality of itself.

Love is the name we give to experience when it reawakens to its identity with all things, when it recognises itself in all things, as all things.

The discovery that peace, happiness and love are ever-present within our own Being, and completely available at every moment of experience, under all conditions, is the most important discovery that anyone can make.

Thought encloses Reality in names; sensations and perceptions enclose it in forms. Divested of these projections, Reality stands as the raw, unnameable, indivisible intimacy of all experience.

Awakening or enlightenment is the experiential understanding that what we essentially are does not share the limits or the destiny of the body or mind.

I, Awareness, can never be seen or known as an object, and yet all thoughts, feelings, sensations and perceptions shine with My light alone.

To begin with I, Awareness, am found as the witness in the background of experience. Then, objects recede into the background and I shine in the foreground of all experience. Then, the apparent distinction and distance between Myself and objects dissolves, and I am found in everything and everyone, and everyone and everything is found in Me.

If we want to learn to live without suffering, we first have to learn to live with it. When suffering is welcomed so completely that there is not the slightest resistance to it, what we were seeking, by trying to get rid of it, is revealed at its heart.

An object is limited from the viewpoint of a subject; a self is limited from the viewpoint of a self. In the absence of a limited viewpoint, all objects and selves are seen and known as they truly are, eternal and infinite.

Just as the activity in a movie is made of the motionless screen, so the agitation of the body and mind is made of the ever-present peace of our essential Being.

At some point, life, love and meditation become indistinguishable.

Have the courage and the clarity to see that God neither cares nor even knows about suffering. Suffering is resistance, and God – eternal, infinite Awareness – like empty space, knows no resistance, and therefore cannot know suffering.

Our essential nature of pure Awareness is like an open window: it makes the viewing possible but is not in the view.

Just as the characters and objects in a movie seem to acquire a reality of their own when their true reality, the screen, is overlooked, so a multiplicity and diversity of objects, selves and others seem to come into existence and acquire a reality of their own when our essential nature of pure Awareness is apparently forgotten, veiled or overlooked.

I, the light of pure Knowing, am the Experiencing in all experience.

Experience is like a piece of cloth, woven with strands of coloured yarn. Thoughts, feelings, sensations and perceptions are like the strands: separate and distinct when we look at the colours but one indivisible whole when we look at the cloth.

Suffering expresses itself as the activity of resisting what is present and seeking what is not present. The separate self is made of that activity.

Thinking imagines that our essential nature of pure Awareness shares the limits and the destiny of the body. With this belief, a limited, temporary self comes into apparent existence, on whose behalf most thoughts, feelings, activities and relationships are undertaken.

Find your Self first as the knower of the known, and then as the Knowing in both.

Love is the experience that others are not others. Beauty is the experience that objects are not objects.

Enlightenment is not *an* experience. It is the revelation of the true nature of *all* experience.

It is our essential nature of pure Knowing that, modulating itself in the form of thinking, seems to become a mind; modulating itself in the form of sensing, seems to become a body; and modulating itself in the form of seeing, hearing, touching, tasting and smelling, seems to become a world; but never is, knows or becomes anything other than itself.

Openness to all experience is not something we, as Awareness, *do*; it is what we *are*.

Thought seems to know a subject (the knower) and an object (the known) but Knowing knows only Knowing. We *are* that Knowing, and thus we know our Self alone.

Love is the dissolution of the 'I' that loves and the 'other' that is loved. It is the collapse of relatedness and the dawn of intimacy.

Happiness or peace is the absence of resistance or seeking.
It is the natural and ever-present condition of our Self,
Awareness, in all situations and under all circumstances.

At its core, the separate self is a shrinking from intimacy with, and openness to, all experience.

Our essential nature of pure Knowing does not know anything separate from itself and, therefore, does not know a separate self, object, other or world. A separate self, object, other or world is only such from the illusory point of view of a separate self.

Don't be an inside self, listening to an outside sound; just be the hearing. Don't be an inside self, seeing an outside world; just be the seeing.

There is no knower of experience and no experience that is known; there is just the knowing of it. In fact, not the knowing 'of it'. We never find the 'it'; we know just Knowing, and it is Knowing that knows only Knowing.

Devotion is love directed towards an 'other'. Divested of the 'other' our devotion finds nothing to turn towards, and, as a result, vacillates for a moment, flows back to its source, and stands revealed as pure love.

Attention is Awareness directed towards an object. Divested of the object, attention, finding nothing to grasp, quivers for a moment, flows back to its source, and stands revealed as pure Awareness.

We are the light of pure Knowing that runs through all experience. Stay with that, as that. Be and know only that.

There are three possibilities in life: to be something, nothing or everything. In the first, there is suffering; in the second, there is peace; and in the third, there is happiness and love.

There is no distance or separation between the world and our experience of it, nor between experience and our Self.

When the 'there' dissolves, the 'here' is revealed. When the 'here' dissolves, I, Awareness, remain.

Thought says that the body and world are solid, lasting and substantial, and that our essential nature of pure Awareness is fleeting and insubstantial. In fact, it is Awareness that is ever-present and substantial, whereas all we know of the body and world is an ever-changing flow of fleeting sensations and perceptions. Thus, the reality that thought attributes to the body and world properly belongs to Awareness alone.

Everything we have ever longed for – peace, happiness and love – resides at the heart of all experience, always available, under all circumstances.

We never truly desire an object for its own sake; we desire only to be relieved of the agitation of resistance and seeking that takes us away from the Now into time. Thus, all we ever truly desire is to be desireless.

I, the light of pure Knowing, do not know a self, object, other or world, as such. I see or know only the indivisible, unnameable intimacy of Experiencing.

It is not necessary to let go of a separate self, but rather to see that there is no separate self.

From the point of view of a separate self there is bondage and liberation, veiling and revealing, seeking and finding, not knowing and knowing. But from the point of view of Myself, pure Awareness, I never fall into bondage and am thus never liberated; I am never veiled from Myself and am, therefore, never revealed; I cannot be lost and am, therefore, never found; I am never not known and, therefore, do not need to be known afresh.

Oneness is one thing too many. Hence, in their wisdom and humility, the ancient sages just said that Reality is 'not-two'.

Know your Self as the Knowing in all that is known.

Ask yourself what has never been, and could never be, parted from you, and remain with that, as that.

Enlightenment is the end of one process – thinking and feeling oneself to be a separate, limited self – but the beginning of another – the realignment of the body, mind and world with this new, experiential understanding.

The separate self is like a character in a movie that travels the world in search of the screen.

Thought does not and cannot know Reality, and yet it is made of it.

The sky doesn't need to get rid of the clouds in order to be the open, empty sky; the screen doesn't need to get rid of an image in order to be the transparent screen. Our Self, Awareness, doesn't need to get rid of any appearance of the mind, body or world in order to rest in and as itself.

From the earth's point of view, the sun shines with varying degrees of brightness, but from its own point of view it always shines with the same intensity. Likewise, from the mind's point of view, there are various degrees or states of Awareness, but from the point of view of Awareness, which is the only real point of view, there are no degrees, levels or states of itself: it is always shining brightly, undiminished, untainted, unobscured by any experience of the body, mind or world, eternally knowing and being its own fullness alone.

If we invest our happiness in an intermittent object, substance, activity, relationship or state, we are, by definition, securing unhappiness for ourselves.

The past is made of memory, the future of imagination. Neither has any existence outside the realm of thought.

Thinking has its home in Me, Awareness, but I do not make My home in it.

Everything we know is known through Awareness; therefore, our knowledge of anything is only as good as our knowledge of Awareness. If we believe that Awareness is limited, experience will appear in accordance with that belief, as a succession of limited, finite objects and selves. If we understand that Awareness is eternal and infinite, everything and everyone will be revealed as such.

'I' stands for indivisible, infinite, intimate and innocent. It is the substance of all experience.

Our essential nature of pure Awareness has no agenda with the mind, body or world. It is like empty space, completely allowing and yet indifferent to whatever appears within it. However, it is not a cold, distant indifference: it gives its substance utterly and intimately to whatever appears within it. As such, it is a loving indifference. Be knowingly this loving indifference.

The separate self is the rejection of the Now. I, Awareness, am in love with the Now. In fact, I *am* the Now.

Every appearance is an impersonal act of creation. Seeing this clearly relieves us of any sense of personal guilt, blame, judgement or responsibility. However, this understanding does not lead to irresponsible or unloving behaviour. On the contrary, it enables the mind and body to function on behalf of impersonal love and intelligence, rather than representing the fears and demands of a non-existent self.

All that is known of a mind, body or world are thoughts, sensations and perceptions. All that is known of thoughts, sensations and perceptions are thinking, sensing and perceiving. All that is known of thinking, sensing and perceiving is the knowing of them. Thus, all that is ever known is Knowing, and it is Knowing that knows itself alone.

Thought doesn't know truth; it dissolves in it. Feeling doesn't find love; it merges in it. Perception doesn't see beauty; it dies in it.

Happiness is what we are, not what we know; unhappiness is what we know, not what we are.

Our essential nature of pure Awareness is utterly surrendered to all experience. It is pure innocence, openness, intimacy, allowing, sensitivity and availability, an unconditional 'Yes' to all experience just as it is from moment to moment, without judgement or preference.

From one point of view, the mind, body and world veil the presence of Awareness, but from another they shine with it, just as an image on a screen can be seen either to veil or reveal the screen.

Reality shines as Awareness in the Self, and as Existence in the world.

Only an apparently inside self knows an apparently outside object, other or world, but I, the light of pure Knowing, know Myself alone.

Everything belongs to everything; everyone belongs to everyone.

Our Self, the light of pure Knowing, never finds, knows or comes in contact with anything other than itself. That is the experience of love and beauty.

Once desire is liberated from the need to produce happiness for a non-existent self, it is revealed as a play of energies that express, share and celebrate happiness itself.

Thinking, sensing and perceiving are made of pure Knowing, but Knowing is not made of thinking, sensing or perceiving.

Don't let thinking divide loving into a lover and the beloved, feeling into a feeler and the felt, seeing into a seer and the seen, hearing into a hearer and the heard, touching into a toucher and the touched, tasting into a taster and the tasted, smelling into a smeller and the smelt, or thinking into a thinker and a thought.

As the witnessing background of all experience, our essential nature of pure Awareness is inherently free from all things; as the substance of all experience, it is intimately one with all things.

From the point of view of finite thought, all things are finite. From the point of view of Myself, infinite Awareness, all apparent things are infinite.

Happiness and the separate entity are mutually exclusive.

Experience is not experienced by something outside of, separate from or other than itself. Nor does experience ever come in contact with anything other than itself, such as a separate, independently existing object, self or world. Experience just experiences itself – one unnameable, indivisible whole, simultaneously knowing and being itself alone.

Love is the natural condition of all experience before thought has divided it into a multiplicity and diversity of objects, selves and others.

The self that seeks Awareness is like a shadow that seeks the sun.

Every time we find ourselves reacting to anyone or anything, we can ask on whose behalf we are reacting. We will nearly always find that it is on behalf of a non-existent self.

All experience happens in our Self, pure Awareness, and all there is in our Self out of which experience can be made *is* our Self. Therefore, just as there is nothing present in a movie other than the screen, so there is nothing present in experience other than our Self. Pure Awareness *is* all experience, and all experience *is* pure Awareness.

It is our Self, luminous, open, empty Awareness, which gives experience its unmistakable reality. What we truly know and love in all experience is the reality of Awareness. It is that alone for which the apparently separate self longs.

I, the light of pure Knowing, cannot and do not know anything other than Myself.

For thought, the knowing of an object takes place 'here' and the being or existence of an object takes place 'there'. But for Awareness, Knowing and Being are one.

The 'am-ness' of Self is the 'is-ness' of things.

If we replace the impulse to avoid uncomfortable feelings with a desire to face and explore them deeply, we find, at their heart, exactly what we were seeking by trying to avoid them.

Locate yourself nowhere; find yourself everywhere.

Individuality means being undivided. It is the unique expression of the undivided whole that each body and mind expresses, and it flourishes when we are relieved of the straightjacket of ignorance – that is, when we stop ignoring our essential nature of pure Awareness.

Happiness is simply to allow everything to be exactly as it is from moment to moment.

From the limited viewpoint of a body, our essential nature of pure Awareness seems limited; from the temporal viewpoint of a mind, it seems temporary; in the absence of a viewpoint, it is as it is, neither limited nor temporary.

The mind that seeks happiness is like a wave that seeks water.

Security and happiness cannot be found in anything that comes and goes. Find whatever it is in your experience that doesn't appear, move, change or disappear, and invest your identity, security and happiness in that alone.

Non-duality is not an immunisation against feeling. In fact, it is the opposite: it is unconditional openness, sensitivity, vulnerability and possibility.

Thought has taken the ever-present reality that properly belongs to Me, Awareness, and superimposed it upon the mind, body and world. Give back to Me what properly belongs to Me, and everything will fall into place.

Just as the singularity of a necklace is derived from one invisible thread on which numerous beads are strung, so it is the single, invisible but ever-present reality of Awareness that gives innumerable perceptions their coherence and continuity, and out of them forms an apparently independent and permanent world.

Pure intimacy, parted by thought, becomes a self and world.

The role of the artist is to transmit to humanity the deepest experience of Reality. Art is remembrance. It is love. It is like a sword that distinguishes between appearances and Reality, or a cradle that reminds us of home.

Once the body is no longer presided over by the tyranny of a separate self, it gradually returns to its natural state of peace, openness, transparency, availability, sensitivity and love.

Happiness is not an experience that I, Awareness, *have*. It is what I *am*.

Happiness is simply the knowing of our own Being – the natural, effortless and innate condition of our Self when it is no longer pulled into an imaginary past or projected into an imaginary future by resistance and seeking.

All we know of a mind, body or world is Experiencing, and Experiencing is so intimate and close as to be indistinguishable from our Self.

Love knows no other. Beauty knows no object.

It is not necessary to get rid of thoughts, images and ideas; just cease deriving your sense of identity from them.

Time is created by thought to accommodate the seeking/resisting activity of the imaginary separate self.

Let thoughts and feelings have their home in you, but don't make your home in them.

What we long for is the space of Awareness in which all longing takes place. In fact, it is even closer than that. What we long for is itself taking the shape of our longing.

I, the light of pure Knowing, am to experience what a screen is to an image.

Pure Knowing, without a subject that knows or an object that is known, is what we *are*, not what we *do*. Thus, for our Self, to know is to be, and to be is to know.

As a separate entity one always feels alone and, as such, life is a process of easing the pain of this loneliness through substances, objects, activities and relationships. As Awareness one is also alone, but only in the sense that there are no others to be either separate from or one with. This is the aloneness of love.

The ultimate purpose of evolution is to draw attention to that which does not evolve.

Bodies and minds don't have Awareness; Awareness has bodies and minds.

At the back of the mind is a doorway with the words 'I am' written above it. First, turn towards that doorway; then walk through it. Turning towards it is an activity of the mind; walking through it is the dissolution of the mind. That dissolution is the revelation of our essential nature of ever-present, unlimited Awareness, the abode of peace, happiness and love.

Awareness does the observing; thought does the judging.

All love is for the Self; all longing is for an object.

There are two possible responses to suffering: one, to go outwards seeking relief in an object, substance, activity, relationship or state; two, to go inwards to the core of our Being. The former may bring temporary relief, but the latter is the abode of lasting peace and happiness.

Happiness appears as desire when it is veiled; desire is revealed as happiness when it is fulfilled.

In ignorance, I am the known; in understanding, I am the knower; in love, I am pure Knowing.

As the witnessing presence of Awareness, we stand in the background of experience; as the light of pure Knowing, we stand at its heart.

At the heart of experience, there is a fire that burns all we know. Offer everything to that fire. What remains – the ashes of love – is that for which we have longed all our life.